THE
COUNTRY LIFE
BOOK OF
ENGLISH CHINA

From the upper left corner reading clockwise: Longton Hall vase, about 1755; Bow sauceboat, about 1755; Bow tankard, about 1760; Liverpool cream or sauce boat, about 1770; Staffordshire creamware squirrel, about 1790; Chelsea seal in the form of a parrot, about 1760; Plymouth sauceboat, about 1770; Worcester tea-caddy, about 1765; Saltglaze bear cup and cover, about 1740; Caughley cream jug, about 1780; Bow figure of a boy, about 1755. *Centre:* Bristol pottery plate inscribed 'Mrs Rogers 1750'.
(All in the collection of the author)

THE COUNTRY LIFE
BOOK OF
ENGLISH CHINA

GEOFFREY WILLS

LONDON : COUNTRY LIFE LIMITED

First published in 1964 by
Country Life Limited,
Tavistock Street, London WC2
Printed in Great Britain by
Hazell Watson & Viney Ltd.,
Aylesbury, Bucks.

Contents

List of Plates

PORCELAIN

Sources of the pieces illustrated are as follows:
Museum of the Royal Institution of Cornwall, Truro: Figs. 2, 3, 17, 18, 22, 23, 25, 26, 33, 34, 36, 38, 41, 42, 43, 44, 45, 47, 49, 50, 55, 60, 64, 70, 71, 72, 79, 80, 82, 84, 85, 86, 87, 88, 90, 93, 94, 95, 96, 97, 101, 105, 106, 107, 119, 122, 123, 125, 128, 132.
City Museum and Art Gallery, Plymouth: Figs. 4, 10, 20, 24, 39, 46, 51, 57, 65, 69, 73, 74, 75, 81, 83, 91, 99, 111, 114, 115, 116, 117, 124, 126, 131.
Victoria and Albert Museum, London: Figs. 1, 5, 6, 40, 52, 53, 76, 129, 130.
The National Trust (Fenton House, Hampstead): Figs. 54, 67, 118.
Josiah Wedgwood & Sons, Ltd, Barlaston, Staffs.: Figs. 31, 35, 37.
Royal Albert Memorial Museum, Exeter: Fig. 7.
Author: Frontispiece; Figs. 8, 9, 11, 12, 13, 14, 15, 16, 19, 21, 27, 28, 29, 30, 32, 48, 56, 58, 59, 61, 62, 63, 66, 68, 77, 78, 89, 92, 98, 100, 102, 103, 104, 108, 109, 110, 112, 113, 120, 121, 127.

Introduction

In this book the word China is deliberately used to describe both Pottery and Porcelain. In simple terms, the difference is that pottery is baked clay, and true porcelain is composed of a baked mixture of particular kinds of ground-up stone and clay (china-stone and china-clay) which combine when heated to a sufficiently high temperature. Alternatively, a type of porcelain, sometimes called 'soft paste' or artificial porcelain, can be made from glass and clay. In England, all except that made at Plymouth and Bristol (pages 86 to 92) was of the 'soft' variety, and the West Country factory founded by William Cookworthy stands alone for having made true porcelain.

The pieces illustrated have been selected to show a range of the different types of china made in England between about 1500 and 1830. In any anthology, whether of the written word or of pictures of objects of art, much has to be omitted for want of space and it is impossible to please every reader or even for the compiler to satisfy himself. In this instance the photographs are reproduced on a large scale, but not larger than their actual size. This makes them of more value, but of course reduces their number and adds to the difficulty of selection. The introductory notes to each section have been kept brief and so have the captions, but each of the latter includes the size of the piece shown and the approximate date of its manufacture.

The presence of marks is noted, but it should be observed that features such as the bases of figures and groups as well as the handles of teapots, sauceboats, cups and tankards are frequently of individual design used by one particular factory or maker. For identifying the origin of specimens these distinctive points can be more helpful than marks which, more often than not, are disappointingly absent.

Acknowledgments

Over one hundred of the photographs have been taken specially for this book, and thanks are due to the following for allowing the photographing of specimens in their care and for assisting in handling them: Mr H. L. Douch, Curator of the Museum of the Royal Institution of Cornwall, Truro; Mr A. A. Cumming, Curator of the City Museum and Art Gallery, Plymouth; and Dr R. C. Blackie, Curator of the Royal Albert Memorial Museum, Exeter. It is appropriate that the majority of the illustrations show pieces from collections in the West Country, whence came supplies of the clay and stone that form the substance of many of the wares.

For use of the remaining photographs thanks are due to: The Director of the Victoria and Albert Museum, London; The National Trust (pieces at Fenton House, Hampstead); Josiah Wedgwood & Sons, Ltd, Barlaston; and for allowing reproduction of illustrations that have appeared in the pages of their journals: Mr L. G. G. Ramsey, F.S.A., Editor of *The Connoisseur*, and Mr Denys Sutton, Editor of *Apollo*.

Factories and Dates

POTTERY

Factories, large and small, were so numerous that it is not possible to give their dates individually. The following is a list of the principal types of ware and the approximate dates during which they were made:

'PEASANT' WARE (lead-glazed): from medieval times to the present day, but the main interest for the collector lies in pieces made during the seventeenth and in the first part of the eighteenth centuries.

DELFTWARE (tin-glazed): from about 1600 until the end of the eighteenth century.

CREAMWARE: from about 1750 this was developed in Staffordshire, and by 1765 Josiah Wedgwood had evolved from it his famous Queen's Ware. It remained popular until gradually ousted by a white-bodied pottery from about 1800.

STONEWARE (salt-glazed): from the last quarter of the seventeenth century for about a hundred years, but it continued to be made for domestic and commercial uses. It is manufactured to-day for such things as drain-pipes, and until recently was used widely for 'stone' ginger-beer bottles. Wedgwood's superior type of stoneware, which he named Jasperware, was introduced about 1775 and is still made by the firm he founded.

PORCELAIN

CHELSEA	1745 to 1784	1745 to 1749	Triangle mark
		1749 to 1752	Raised anchor
		1753 to 1757	Red anchor
		1758 to 1769	Gold anchor
		1770 to 1784	Chelsea-Derby
'GIRL IN A SWING'	1749 to 1754		
BOW	after 1745 to 1775 or 1776		
DERBY	1750 to 1848	1784 to 1811 crowned 'D' and batons mark: the 'Crown Derby' period	
LUND'S BRISTOL	1749 to 1752		
WORCESTER	1751 to the present day	1751 to 1783 'Dr Wall' period 1783 onwards (see page 66)	
LONGTON HALL	1749 to 1760		
LIVERPOOL	about 1756 to 1840		
LOWESTOFT	1757 to 1802		
CAUGHLEY	1772 to 1814		
PLYMOUTH	1768 to 1770		
BRISTOL	1770 to 1781		
NEW HALL	1781 until about 1835		
COALPORT	about 1797		
MINTONS	about 1798 to the present day		
SPODE	about 1800, bought in 1833 by W. T. Copeland and continued under that name		
NANTGARW AND SWANSEA	1813 to 1822		
ROCKINGHAM	about 1820 to 1842		

1. Middle Bronze Age burial urn decorated by pressing cord on to the damp clay before firing. Excavated at
Bere Regis, Dorset. 10½ inches high.

Pottery

MEDIEVAL TO TUDOR

A surprisingly large quantity of pottery dating back some hundreds of years has survived the passage of time, and most museums in London and elsewhere exhibit specimens from their immediate vicinity and farther afield. It will be seen that both shaping and decoration are simple, the use of a coating of glaze not only enhancing the appearance of an article, but proving essential if it were to be watertight.

The glaze contained some oxide of lead as an ingredient and for that reason pieces covered in it, which continued to be manufactured commercially into the nineteenth century, are described sometimes as 'lead-glazed'. Additions of certain substances (manganese, copper, etc.) produced coloured glazes. A completely glass-like and colourless glaze was not obtainable because of the presence of impurities which defied removal, and an amber tint was the nearest to it that was achieved.

Sometimes designs were cut into the soft clay, before it was put in the kiln for baking and hardening, by impressing it with a piece of cord (Fig. 1), or with an instrument. At a later date, a flat surface, such as that of a tile, could be moulded with a pattern cut in wood or stone (Fig. 3).

2. Tall jug covered in a green glaze on the outside and with a clear glaze inside, the edge of the base impressed with a pattern of finger-prints. Early sixteenth century. Excavated at Nottingham. 11 inches high.

3. Yellow-glazed tile with a raised design showing the Tudor Rose beneath a crown flanked by the initials of Queen Elizabeth I, with her coat-of-arms and supporters. Late sixteenth century. 13½ by 10 inches.

'PEASANT' WARE

These red and white clay pieces were the immediate successors to the preceding, and ample supplies of clay and fuel led to their manufacture concentrating eventually in Staffordshire. Whereas earlier pottery had been fired with wood, of which enormous quantities were needed for the purpose, this became scarce and from about the middle of the seventeenth century coal was used increasingly. The noticeably simple modelling and decoration has led to this type of pottery being labelled conveniently 'peasant' ware. Various types of ornament were popular, especially those using 'slip'— clay in liquid form which could be applied to a piece like sugar-icing to a cake (Figs 4, 5 and 6).

4. Staffordshire red clay dish with cream-coloured slip decoration, inscribed
RALPH SIMSON. About 1700. 17 inches diameter.

Slip of a contrasting colour was used also to cover an article completely and was then scratched through to show the design in the colour of the under-surface. This technique is called 'sgraffito', from the Italian, and potteries in the West of England, at Barnstaple and elsewhere, specialised in making such pieces until quite recent times (Fig. 7).

Some of the Staffordshire potters inscribed the names of their friends or of themselves on their work, and those of the Toft, Shaw and Simpson families (often mis-spelled as in Fig. 4), and others have been noted. In Kent, Wrotham was another important potting centre, many pieces from there bearing initials and dates between about 1600 and 1750 (Fig. 6).

Many of the surviving specimens of 'peasant' ware are elaborate in both shape and ornament, and their decorative quality has ensured their careful treatment. Most of them were made as gifts for special occasions, usually local ones: young potters presented them to their sweethearts; and weddings, christenings (Fig. 5), and other family events were celebrated. They were sometimes treasured as heirlooms long after whatever occasioned their making had been forgotten, and half a century or so ago examples were to be found in the cottages of Staffordshire and elsewhere in the vicinity of old potteries. The rougher wares made for everyday use, simple in design and plain in appearance, have nearly all disappeared.

5. Staffordshire cream-coloured clay cradle with red slip decoration, made as a christening gift. About 1700. 10¾ inches long.

6. Wrotham (Kent) red and cream clay three-handled cup, known as a 'Tyg', dated 1621. 6⅝ inches high.

7. West Country red and cream-coloured clay Harvest jug with sgraffito decoration. 14 inches high. Under the handle it is inscribed:

'Harvis is cam all bissey
Now in mackin of your
Barly mow when men do
Laber hard and swet good
Ale is better far than meet
Bideford   April 28
1775   M—W.'

DELFTWARE

This type of pottery takes its name from the Dutch town, the centre of the potting industry in Holland, where the Italian method of coating pieces with a glaze rendered opaque by the use of an oxide of tin was practised. The glaze on top of ordinary clay gave a white surface which could be painted in a range of colours, and was a great advance over the transparent lead glazes otherwise employed. Pieces decorated in this manner are referred to sometimes as 'tin-glazed' or as 'delftware'; the latter with a small 'd' to distinguish them from Dutch-made Delftware.

8. Charger decorated in colours showing Adam and Eve and the Serpent. About 1650. 15¾ inches diameter.

The process was used in England by 1600 and during the whole of the seventeenth and eighteenth centuries. Important centres of manufacture were in London, notably at Lambeth, where there were a number of potteries, and at Liverpool, Bristol, Wincanton (Somerset) and Dublin. It is thought, not unreasonably, that specimens painted with the coats-of-arms of City Companies were made in London (Figs 10 and 11).

Tin-glazed pottery is recognised easily by the fact that raw edges, underneath plates and jugs for instance, reveal the rough clay forming the body of the article. The fact that the glaze is liable to chip away in use is seen in a large proportion of surviving pieces which have damaged rims (Figs 13 and 16 for instance). This unfortunate weakness led to its replacement by the less-vulnerable cream-ware and by porcelain.

While some delftware was decorated in attractive bright red, green, yellow, brown and blue, much was painted in blue alone in imitation of imported Chinese porcelain, which was copied not only in colour, but also in shape and in the range of subjects depicted. Most of the output was of pieces for use at the table, and plates survive in large numbers. Big dishes, known as chargers and made more for decoration than for use (Fig. 8), were produced throughout the seventeenth century, and punch-bowls (Fig. 13) were popular from after about 1700.

9. Dish commemorating the coronation of King William III and Queen Mary, painted in blue, with 'portraits' and initials. About 1689. 8½ inches diameter.

10. Slab for grinding pills, painted in blue, with the arms of the Apothecaries' Society of London. The motto may be translated: 'Throughout the world I am called the bringer of aid'. Late seventeenth century. $10\frac{1}{4}$ inches high.

11. Tankard, painted in blue, with the arms of the Blacksmiths' Company of London. Inscribed: 'Brother Vilckin Let Us Drink Whilst Wee Have Breath For There's No Drinking AFter Death: Joseph Piper: 1752'. $7\frac{1}{4}$ inches high.

12. Bristol plate, painted in colours, with a seated Chinese figure. About 1750. 9 inches diameter.

13. Punch-bowl, painted in blue, with Oriental designs and inscribed under the base: 'june the 27th 1758'. 9 inches diameter.

14. Vase with 'mimosa' pattern painted in blue. About 1750. 7 inches high.

15. Liverpool wall-tile printed in black. Late eighteenth century. 4¾ inches square.

16. Eighteenth-century ointment pot, dug out of a garden in 1962. 2 inches diameter.

STONEWARE

Stoneware was imported into England from Germany from the sixteenth century, and took the form of jugs and drinking-vessels. They are of a whitish-grey colour, their composition being clay fired to a very high temperature and glazed, when considered necessary, by the simple method of throwing a quantity of common salt into the kiln while the ware was baking. The resulting product, known as 'salt-glazed stoneware', is a distinctive material with a thin glaze that does not obscure any pattern on it, and that often has a finely-pitted surface comparable with that of orange peel (Fig. 19).

John Dwight of Fulham was granted a patent for making an English imitation of the German product in 1671, and a few pieces undoubtedly of his manufacture have survived. His pottery was carried on by successive owners, and among their specialities were tankards with raised ornaments further decorated with washes of brown-tinted clay (Fig. 19). Brown-coloured wares were made also in Nottingham from about 1700 (Fig. 18) and in other places.

In Staffordshire, improvements were made in stoneware in order to compete with porcelain, and a whiter variety was evolved by about 1730. Unusual and attractive designs were produced and colouring was attempted with success. This was either in a full range with a rich pink and a turquoise-blue predominating, or in what is termed 'scratch blue'—a pattern being scratched in the clay and dusted with powdered blue pigment (Fig. 22). Another variety of stoneware is dark red in colour; it originated in China where teapots of the material were made and exported with consignments of tea. The idea that the beverage tasted better and was more beneficial when brewed in a redware pot came into favour, and Dwight as well as two Dutch brothers who came to England, John and David Elers, were prominent in making a pottery of this type (Fig. 17). It was made also in Germany and Holland, and it is difficult to be certain in some instances where the surviving pieces originated.

17. Unglazed red stoneware mug with raised decoration of a sprig of blossom. About 1700. $3\frac{1}{2}$ inches high.

18. Nottingham brown-glazed mug with pierced ornament. About 1700. $4\frac{1}{8}$ inches high.

19. Fulham tankard coloured in shades of brown and decorated with a bust of
Queen Anne and a huntsman with hounds and a stag. Inscribed round the top:
'Drink to the Pious Memory of Good Queen Ann, July y^e 25: 1729' (Queen
Anne died in 1714). 8¼ inches high.

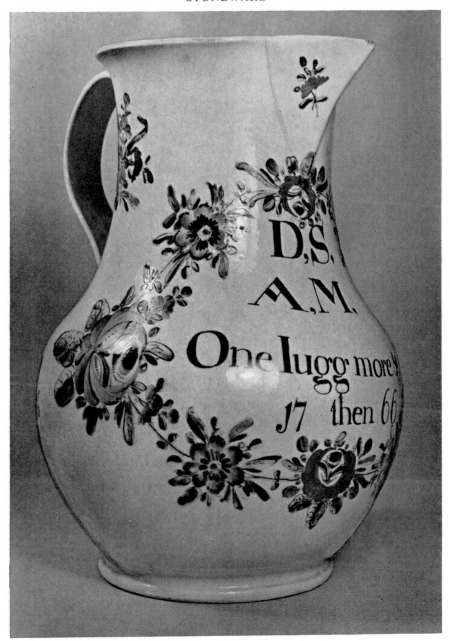

20. Jug with a coloured design of flowers, initials and the curious wording: 'One Iugg more and then 1766'. 7¾ inches high.

21. Cup and cover in the form of a bear seated hugging a dog, the fur of the animals imitated with shreds of clay. About 1740. 3¼ inches high.

22. Hollow 'brick' with a pierced top and 'scratch-blue' decoration. Filled with sand, it would have served as a stand for quill pens, and filled with water for flowers. About 1750. 6¾ inches long.

23. Sauceboat moulded with a pattern of scrolls on a chequered ground, the former coloured. About 1750. 8½ inches long.

24. Teapot painted in white on a dark blue ground. About 1750. 6¾ inches long.

CREAMWARE

The search for better products with which to meet the increasing competition of porcelain led to the introduction about the middle of the eighteenth century of a ware with a cream-coloured body. This was developed from the white clay, often used in the form of 'slip' and familiar to the makers of 'peasant' pieces for a century or more (Figs 4, 5, 6 and 7); the name of Thomas Astbury is associated with the improvement. This creamware was covered in transparent coloured lead glazes which were usually dabbed on to give a blotched effect that is far more pleasing than it sounds.

The foremost potter in the evolution of this ware and its glazes was Thomas Whieldon, but he did not mark his productions and positive identification is seldom possible. He was followed by two men, father and son, both named Ralph Wood, whose figures and groups have achieved for them a lasting fame (Figs 28 and 30). This is not only because of the originality of the models, but because they were the first to control the colours carefully and give them a more natural effect (compare Fig. 26 with 28). A small proportion of the Woods' pieces are marked with a stamp bearing their names, and others have a tiny raised representation of a group of trees—a punning play on their surname.

26. A Turk, streaked with brown and green glazes. About 1750. 5¾ inches high.

25. Figure of a seated cat with brown and olive-green markings. About 1750. 4 inches high.

27. Plate decorated with glazes of brown, green and grey to give the effect of tortoiseshell. About 1760. $9\frac{3}{4}$ inches diameter.

28. A flute-player with a shepherdess and animals, made by Ralph Wood and
decorated with coloured glazes. About 1775. $9\frac{3}{4}$ inches high.

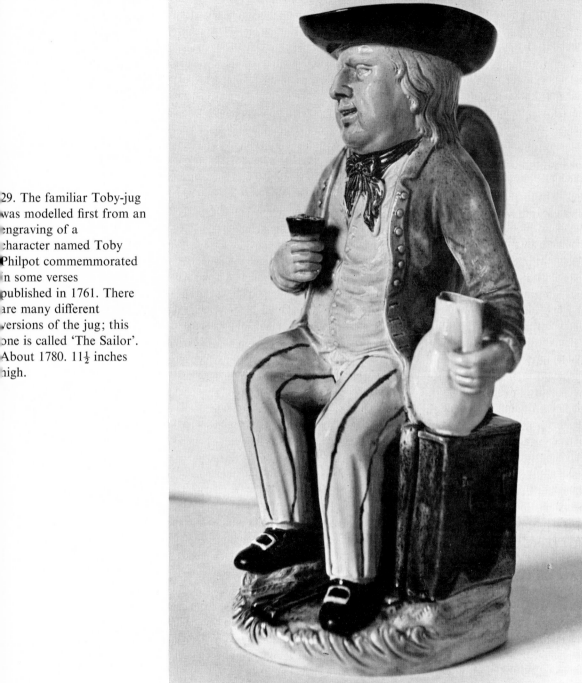

29. The familiar Toby-jug was modelled first from an engraving of a character named Toby Philpot commemmorated in some verses published in 1761. There are many different versions of the jug; this one is called 'The Sailor'. About 1780. 11½ inches high.

30. Group of a terrier baiting a bull; at the back is stamped 'Ra. Wood'. About 1775. 5¾ inches high. This group is typical of the work of the Woods; the pale-coloured washes of glaze with a brilliant sheen accentuating the neat potting. Other homely subjects, sporting and otherwise, were modelled, and the makers appealed to a more cultured market with figures of gods and goddesses decorated in a similar manner.

WEDGWOOD

Josiah Wedgwood merits a section to himself in any consideration of eighteenth-century English pottery. He spread the fame of Staffordshire throughout the world, and by his skill, industry and inventiveness both his own name and the firm he founded have endured to the present day. He was in partnership with Thomas Whieldon for a few years, but by 1759 had started his own pottery where he made wares of types similar to those of his neighbours and competitors. Although unmarked, Wedgwood's are recognised by their superior potting and the greater brilliance of their glazes (Figs 33 and 34).

31. Josiah Wedgwood, 1730–1795, modelled when he was 47 years old.

In 1765, a cream-coloured ware, which he evolved from the creamwares of Whieldon and the Woods (pages 30 to 34), was named 'Queen's Ware' after Queen Charlotte had purchased some pieces of it. In a short time this became immensely popular and, whether entirely plain or with sparse but tasteful decoration, was to be found in homes in every known land.

As the result of a friendship with a Liverpool man, Thomas Bentley, who had a keen appreciation of the Antique with which Wedgwood became inspired, the two men formed a partnership. A new factory named Etruria was built at Burslem in 1769, and here were made the special types of stoneware with which the name of Wedgwood is linked: basaltes named after the black stone it resembles, and the series of coloured jasperwares used to make the well-known vases, plaques and other pieces ornamented with reliefs. The most famous of these are undoubtedly the copies of the Portland Vase, of which the original is in the British Museum, begun in 1786 and not finished until four years later (Fig. 37). Fewer than twenty of the first series of copies have been located, but large numbers of less carefully made ones have been turned out subsequently. Until Bentley's death in 1780 the names of both men were stamped on their Etruria productions, but creamware has that of Wedgwood alone and so have jasperwares and basaltes made after 1780.

The firm of Wedgwood still makes many thousands of pieces each year in the old patterns, as it has done continuously since the time of Josiah, and it is not always easy for the inexperienced to tell old from new, or from copies made in the nineteenth century. It is helpful to know that since about 1760 the majority of pieces have been marked, and this makes it easy to distinguish the work of the many copyists (Fig. 39). One point is worth remembering—specimens stamped with the word ENGLAND as well as WEDGWOOD were made after 1891, when an American law required imports to bear the name of the country of origin.

32. Jasperware buttons. About 1780. Approximately ⅝ inch high. Like most of Wedgwood's productions these were made for use; among the items manufactured in jasperware were small pieces such as beads, seals and scent-bottles, as well as plaques for mounting, in polished steel or precious metals, as brooches, buckles and watch-cases.

33. Teapot in the form of a pineapple, covered in green and yellow glazes. About 1760. 4½ inches high.

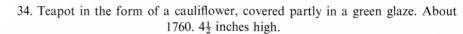

34. Teapot in the form of a cauliflower, covered partly in a green glaze. About 1760. 4½ inches high.

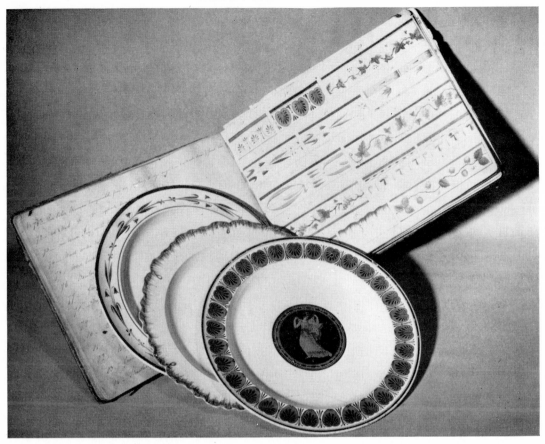

35. A group of decorated Queen's Ware plates, marked WEDGWOOD, with Josiah Wedgwood's original pattern-book of 1770. Plates, 10 inches diameter.

36. Blue and white jasperware butter-dish, cover and stand, marked WEDGWOOD. About 1785. Stand, $6\frac{7}{8}$ inches diameter.

37. The Portland Vase. The original, which is made of dark blue and white Roman glass, has been reproduced many times since the late eighteenth century. This was Josiah Wedgwood's own copy, made under his supervision in 1790. 10 inches high.

38. Red (*Rosso antico*) and black (*Basaltes*) stoneware milk jug, marked WEDGWOOD. About 1820. 5¾ inches long.

39. Black stoneware tea-kettle, unmarked. Made by one of Wedgwood's many imitators, perhaps Humphrey Palmer of Hanley. About 1790. 7¼ inches high.

LEEDS

The pottery at Leeds in Yorkshire made a creamware similar in appearance to that popularised by Josiah Wedgwood. Decoration often took the form of moulded scrolled borders and carefully finished pierced patterns (Fig. 40). Much of the output was left uncoloured, but painted pieces are often in a combination of brownish-red and black (Fig. 41).

Some of the ware is indistinguishable from that made by potters in Staffordshire, Liverpool and elsewhere, but a small proportion bears the mark LEEDS POTTERY, which is found sometimes stamped twice in the form of a cross. The factory continued in production until 1878 and made copies of its earlier pieces which have deceived many collectors.

40. Creamware butter-dish with cover and stand, the knob appropriately in the form of a cow and the cover decorated with a pierced pattern. About 1790. Stand, 7¼ inches long.

41. Creamware teapot with coloured decoration. About 1780. 5 inches high.

EARLY NINETEENTH CENTURY

The early years of the nineteenth century saw new factories opening and old ones continuing to develop. The greatest improvement was the making of a white-bodied glazed earthenware which was decorated, usually in blue, by means of printed patterns (see page 65). It was well made, but intended to be sold cheaply, and the firms of Spode and Wedgwood competed with dozens of others in Staffordshire and elsewhere to supply eager buyers on both sides of the Atlantic. Almost as popular were the Stone-china of Spode and Mason's Ironstone China, both of which were very durable; the latter was usually decorated floridly with Oriental designs in red and vivid blue.

More for decoration than utility were pieces covered in lustre glazes—copper (Figs 43 and 44) and silver—which continue to be made to the present day. Mantelpiece ornaments differed little in design from those of earlier date, but their colours were more garish, with the pale washes of lead glaze supplanted by realistic painting in harsher shades applied on top of a clear glaze (Figs 45 and 46). A few factories continued to make wares of a higher quality than the average, and among these Swansea is noteworthy (Fig. 42).

42. Swansea plate painted in colours, the name of the plant 'Dwarf Orchis' written in red on the back. About 1800. 7¾ inches diameter.

43. Staffordshire goblet decorated in copper lustre. About 1830. 5 inches high.

44. Staffordshire jug moulded with figures of sportsmen with a dog, and painted in colours and lustre. About 1820. 5½ inches high.

45. Staffordshire figure of a youth painted in colours over the glaze. About 1800.
$8\frac{1}{2}$ inches high.

46. Staffordshire figure of a seated lion. About
1825. 4¼ inches high.

47. Bristol puzzle-jug with coloured decoration.
About 1820. 5 inches high.

48. Plate printed in blue with an imaginary landscape, impressed mark:
SPODE. About 1810. 10 inches diameter.

Porcelain

CHELSEA

The factory was in existence by 1745; a few cream jugs have survived which are incised beneath the base with that date, a triangle and the word 'Chelsea'. Other pieces marked with a triangle alone are known, and all share a pleasant milk-white appearance and a shining glaze.

By 1749 announcements in newspapers linked the name of a Belgian-born silversmith, Nicholas Sprimont, with the factory. He was manager for a few years, and after 1758 became proprietor. From 1749 pieces were marked with a small anchor moulded on a raised oval pad (can this choice of emblem be attributed to the Thames-side situation of the works?), but soon the raised anchor was outlined in red (Fig. 52). Then, from 1753 to 1757, it was painted direct in red on a flat part of the object, and often is so insignificant as to be overlooked.

Pieces with the triangle or raised anchor are rare, and both marks are found mostly on useful articles such as salt-cellars, cups and saucers and teapots. A few figures were made, and like the other pieces were sometimes left unpainted. The red anchor period saw the finest of Chelsea porcelain, and the figures and groups have been described with reason as being among the best made in all Europe. While many were copied from Dresden originals (Fig. 53), others were completely new, and the creation of some of them has been discovered recently to have been the work of another Belgian-born craftsman, a man named Joseph Willems who was known here by his anglicised surname of Williams.

The final period, which began in about 1758, was notable for the use of lavish decoration both in painting and gilding. The mark was an anchor in gold, and productions included elaborately designed vases as well as figures and groups.

Mention must be made of the famous miniature pieces often known now by their eighteenth-century name of 'Toys'—a word that did not then mean only children's playthings, but trifles. They included not only seals and scent-bottles, but snuff-boxes, needle-cases, pipe-stoppers and similar small-sized articles that are usually more decorative than useful, but are nonetheless delightful.

Sprimont sold the factory in 1769, and eventually it was bought by William Duesbury of Derby, who carried it on until 1784. During his ownership a mark in the form of a capital 'D' combined with an anchor was used.

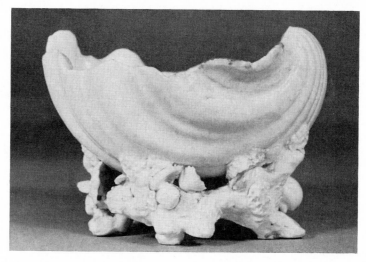

49. Salt-cellar moulded as a scallop shell on a base of coral and sea-shells. About 1750. 3¼ inches long.

50. Cream jug modelled with two seated goats and with a bee, known as a 'Goat and Bee' jug, marked with a triangle incised under the base. About 1745. 4¼ inches high.

51. Box and cover in the form of an apple with a caterpillar for the handle, marked inside the lid with a small anchor in red. About 1755. 4 inches high.

52. Figure of a warbler, marked with a raised anchor outlined in red (visible to the
right of the base). About 1750. $5\frac{1}{4}$ inches high.

53. Group of a woman dancing with a masked man, copied from a Dresden original of about 1740 and marked with an anchor in red. About 1755. 7 inches high.

54. Figures of a shepherd and a shepherdess, marked with an anchor in gold. About 1760. 11 and $11\frac{1}{2}$
inches high.

55. Plate painted in the centre with an
exotic bird, the border with coloured
flowers and with insects in gold on
panels of deep blue, marked with an
anchor in gold. Of similar design
to plates in a service given by
George III and Queen Charlotte to
the brother of the latter, the Duke
of Mecklenburg-Strelitz, in 1763.
$8\frac{3}{4}$ inches diameter.

56. A group of 'Toys': (Left to right) Snuff-box modelled with a boy playing a flute with sheep beside him;
scent-bottle designed as fish in a net; three seals, that on the right representing the Marquis of Granby.
All about 1760. Box, $2\frac{3}{4}$ inches long; bottle, $3\frac{3}{4}$ inches high; seals, $1\frac{1}{4}$ inches high.

'GIRL IN A SWING' FACTORY

A number of figures and groups with details in common have been assumed to be the productions of a rival factory to Sprimont's, situated also in Chelsea, working between about 1749 and 1754. A noted example is a figure of a girl seated on a swing between two trees, and the whole series of pieces, of which fewer than one hundred have so far come to light, is known as the 'girl in a swing' type (Fig. 57).

It has been shown recently that this 'second Chelsea' factory made 'Toys', and it has been suggested that the idea of making miniature pieces in England originated at the rival factory and was copied later by Sprimont.

57. Group of Europa and the Bull of 'Girl in a Swing' type. About 1750. 6½ inches high.

BOW

The starting of the factory at Stratford-le-Bow, in the east of London, was the result of patents taken out in 1744 and 1749 by Thomas Frye (Fig. 58). He was a versatile Irishman, who painted portraits and miniatures and made engravings, and became manager of the factory when it opened sometime after 1745 until he retired in 1759.

Much of the output was of pieces decorated in blue for everyday use at the table. Figures and groups included many copying those imported from Dresden and others of distinctively original design, among them some that were quite as decorative as any made elsewhere. On the whole, however, the porcelain made at Bow is less sophisticated in appearance and only rarely as well finished as that of its rival, Chelsea, but it has an undeniable honest charm that has earned it popularity for two hundred years.

As was the case with other factories, many of the earliest examples were left white and uncoloured, but later ones were usually painted. An opaque middle shade of blue was very popular when contrasted with lemon-yellow, the bases of groups and figures were often lined in a purplish-red, and gilding was applied sparingly in most instances. There was no regular factory mark, but figures sometimes have an anchor and a dagger painted in red, or a blue crescent under the base; the latter is sometimes confused with the similar Worcester crescent, but figures from the latter factory were never marked. Many Bow figures have a square hole at the back for the insertion of a metal candle-holder.

The factory closed in either 1775 or 1776.

58. Engraved self-portrait of Thomas Frye, 1710–1762.

THE BOW CHINA WAREHOUSE was opened on Wednesday last, near the Royal Exchange, in Cornhill, with a back Door facing the Bank in Threadneedle-Street, for the Convenience of all Customers, both in Town and Country, where it will continue to be sold in the same Manner as formerly at Bow, with Allowance made to wholesale Dealers.

59. From a newspaper of February, 1753.

60. An actress in Turkish costume. About 1750. 8½ inches high.

61. Plate with a design copied from Chinese porcelain painted in blue. About 1750. 9 inches diameter.

62. Tankard, painted in blue, with an English version of an Oriental scene. About 1755. 5 inches high.

63. Sauceboat moulded with flowers and decorated with gilding. About 1755. $8\frac{3}{4}$ inches long.

64. Group of a woman and a child bearing sheaves of corn, symbolical of
Summer. About 1760. 7½ inches high.

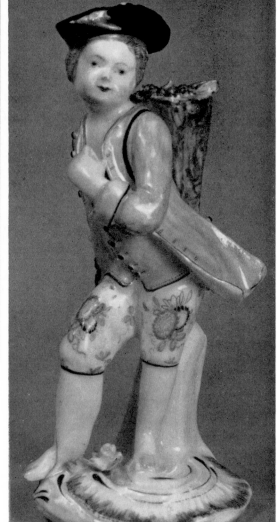

65. Candlestick modelled with a kneeling figure of Cupid reaching up to a bird nesting in a bush. About 1765. 9¾ inches high.

66. Figure of a boy carrying a pannier of grapes, perhaps symbolising Autumn. About 1760. 6¼ inches high.

67. A gardener and his companion, symbolising Autumn and Spring. About 1770. 12½ and 13 inches high.

DERBY

As at Chelsea, cream jugs are the first wares that can be regarded with certainty as having been made at Derby. A few have survived which bear the word 'Derby' or an initial 'D' and the date 1750 on them, and some figures and groups have been identified also as productions of the years between 1750 and 1756. These latter pieces are unmarked, but have some features in common with one another, including a peculiarly dry outer edge at the base and, unless left white, were decorated in pale colours.

In 1756 the factory came into the ownership of William Duesbury, who had worked for some years in London decorating porcelain bought from various sources. Under his direction Derby became noted for figures and groups which were advertised in newspapers of the time as 'the second Dresden'.

The white unglazed ware known as 'biscuit' was introduced about 1770 (Fig. 74). As there was neither glaze nor colouring to conceal roughness or defects each specimen had to be finished with especial care and, in consequence, was sold at a higher price than a comparable coloured one. Derby grew celebrated also for the ornamental vases, services and cabinet cups and saucers that were painted with minute care in a variety of patterns. These and the later groups and figures show many signs of the Classical taste that became fashionable from about 1770. Honeysuckle blossom and other Grecian *motifs* appeared in the borders of plates, and bases composed of scrolls and shells were replaced by those of severely plain type (Figs 74 and 75).

Following his death in 1786 Duesbury was succeeded by his son, also named William, and in 1811 the factory was sold to its manager, Robert Bloor. The quality of its products then began to decline and the concern closed in 1848.

While the earliest figures have the 'dry edge' noted above, later ones invariably show under the base three round marks where they stood on pads in the kiln. Their colouring is lively, and frequently includes a turquoise blue that tends to flake off or turn brown with age. After about 1770 figures were marked with a pattern number incised under the base, and from the time when the Chelsea factory was bought by Duesbury, the mark of a 'D' combined with an anchor was used. Following the closing of the London works in 1784, a mark showing a pair of crossed batons, some dots and a crowned 'D' was painted in red or blue. It was in use until 1811 and gave its name to the so-called 'Crown Derby' period.

AT WILLIAMS's Cool Retreat, formerly Oliver Cromwell's Palace, facing Craig's Court, Charing-cross, being remarkably cooler than most Houses in London, There will be sold by Hand, a few Days longer, all the Remainder of his large Collection of Foreign China, with several new Chinese Curiosities never before exposed to Sale; with great Variety of India Japan Dressing-Boxes in compleat and other Sets; Japan Dressing Glasses, and a large Quantity of new-fashion'd Fans; there is also the greatest Variety of the Derby Porcelain or second Dresden Figures, Baskets, Leaves, &c. and several curious Pieces for Deserts, all mark'd by the Proprietor's Orders at the lowest Prices, with good Allowance to Dealers; several of the said Goods will be sold under prime Cost, rather than risque the moving; for Conveniency of Gentlemen and Ladies Carriages, the Door will be open'd in Spring-Gardens.

68. From a newspaper of 1757.

69. Figure of a street-seller. About 1755. 5 inches high. The man carries a basket holding bottles of absinthe, and he is one of a series of Paris street-sellers copied from some made at Meissen (Dresden) in 1753. The German porcelain factory exported much of its output, and the figures were doubtless made to be sold in France. This English example has the typical dry edge round the base and is decorated in the pale colours used at Derby before about 1760.

70. Figure of a canary perced on a base decorated with flowers. About 1760. $5\frac{1}{4}$ inches high.

71. A sauceboat with floral decoration in colours. About 1770. $7\frac{1}{2}$ inches long.

72. Stand for sweetmeats or pickles. About 1760. 9 inches high.

73. A sportsman with his dog. About 1770. 10¾ inches high.

74. A figure, in the white unglazed ware called 'biscuit', of a gardener, symbolising the element Earth. About 1775. 6½ inches high.

75. Pair of figures of a ewe and a ram. About 1780. 2½ inches high.

76. Covered vase decorated with panels of subjects in grey on a gold-striped
ground, marked with a crowned 'D' in gold. One of a set of three. About
1780. 13⅛ inches high.

LUND'S BRISTOL AND WORCESTER

It was found, perhaps by William Cookworthy (page 86), that the use of Cornish soapstone as an ingredient made an excellent porcelain. A factory for exploiting this discovery was opened in Bristol in 1749 by a man named Benjamin Lund; a factory known until recently by the name of a former occupant, a glassmaker called Lowdin, but which is now referred to more correctly as Lund's. In 1752 the factory and its secrets were acquired by a newly-formed company in Worcester, and the Bristol venture came to an end. One of the partners in the Midlands enterprise was a local physician of some eminence, Dr John Wall, who is remembered for giving his name to the china made at the factory during his lifetime and for some years following his death in 1776.

The wares made during the short period at Bristol include a few surviving figures and sauceboats with the word BRISTOLL embossed on them, and a quantity of tableware (cups, jugs and so forth) particularly delicately painted in blue or in other colours. Decoration was sparse but attractive, and was mostly of Oriental subjects.

Much of the early Worcester output was painted in blue, but by 1757 a new process made it possible to produce decorated ware cheaply. It is uncertain who actually discovered that a design printed on a special thin paper with special ink might be transferred to a piece of china, but some Worcester jugs with a portrait of the king of Prussia bear the date 1757 (Fig. 83). Thereafter printed decoration took its place alongside hand-painting, which remained in use for the better types of ware. By 1760 printing in blue under the glaze was in use, and again Worcester led the field, although other factories were quick to copy the idea.

The Dr Wall period of Worcester, which lasted roughly from 1752 to 1783, was notable for the high quality of its productions both in potting and in decoration. Tablewares and vases were the main output, although some figures were made between 1769 and 1771 and are now extremely rare (Fig. 87). Painting often took the form of shaped panels of exotic birds, figures or landscapes on grounds of various colours: blue, red, yellow, green, etc., some of which were drawn in the form of small scales and others were used in thick, even washes (Figs 84, 85 and 86). Gilding was distinctive, thick and rather dull, and is the feature that usually reveals a fake.

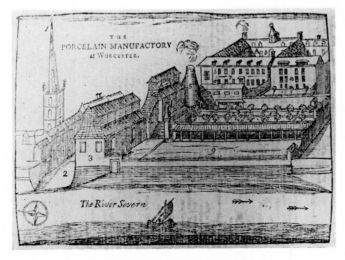

77. 'N.B. A sale of this manufacture will begin at the Worcester muſic meeting on Sept. 20, with great variety of ware, and, 'tis said, at a moderate price'.
From the *Gentleman's Magazine*, August, 1752.

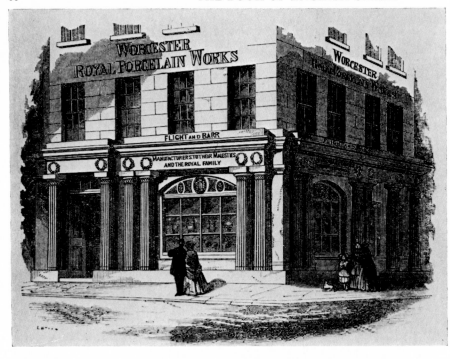

78. The London showroom of the Worcester factory at No. 1, Coventry Street. A woodcut illustration from a book published in 1865.

In 1783 the factory was sold to its London agent, Thomas Flight, and during the ensuing years changed its style from time to time, as follows:

1783–1792	Flight's	1807–1813	Barr, Flight & Barr
1792–1807	Flight & Barr	1813–1840	Flight, Barr & Barr

Under these various owners the high quality of workmanship remained and the fashionable Classical style prevailed (Figs 124 and 128).

Soon after 1783 one of the painters, Humphrey Chamberlain, left the firm and founded one of his own, which in due course absorbed the original company and is in existence to-day.

Marks used in the Wall period included a fretted Chinese-looking square, an imitation of the Dresden crossed swords, the letter 'W', a crescent, and imitation Oriental characters, all in blue. Later pieces have either initials, such as F.B.B. for Flight, Barr & Barr, or a printed mark with name, address and other details in full. Chamberlain's ware was marked some-time with the name of the maker in red.

79. A small example of Lund's Bristol sauceboat with moulded and coloured decoration. About 1750. $4\frac{3}{8}$ inches long.

80. Lund's Bristol sauceboat with moulded and coloured decoration. About 1750. 7¾ inches long.

81. Lund's Bristol double-lipped sauceboat with moulded and coloured decoration, the handles topped with animals' heads. The shapes of this and Figs 79 and 80 are copied from silver originals. About 1750. 8¾ inches long.

82. Tankard with a Chinese landscape painted in a panel on a pale yellow ground. About 1765.
5¾ inches high.

83. Tankard with a portrait of Frederick the Great, King of Prussia, printed in black. Dated 1757. $4\frac{5}{8}$ inches high.

84. Cup and saucer with painted fruit and insects within a pea-green border. About 1775. Saucer, 5¼ inches diameter.

85. Cup and saucer with fruit and flowers painted within a claret-red and gilt border. About 1775. Saucer, 4¾ inches diameter.

86. Flower-holder with panels of flowers and an exotic bird painted on a scale-blue ground, marked with a fretted square in blue. About 1770. 6¾ inches high.

87. A sportswoman, one of the few figures made at Worcester between 1769 and 1771. It is unmarked, as are all the other known specimens. $7\frac{1}{4}$ inches high.

88. Plate with fruit and insects painted by an 'outside decorator': a man who bought china in the white from a factory and decorated it to his own taste or to the order of his clients. About 1775. $8\frac{3}{4}$ inches diameter.

89. Teapot, painted with a Japanese pattern, having a typical Worcester floral knob on the cover and marked with imitation Oriental characters in blue. About 1770. $6\frac{1}{4}$ inches high.

LONGTON HALL

This china works was started in 1749 and lasted for about ten years, but its existence was forgotten completely until some newspaper announcements of the 1750's were discovered and reprinted in 1881. A book on the subject of the factory, published in 1957, told of the dramatic finding of some of the original documents relating to its founding and the result of excavations on the actual site.

The porcelain has been called 'heavy and cold in tone' and the glaze compared with candle-wax, but specimens vary in appearance. They were not always very well finished; flaws that appeared in the kiln during preliminary firing were ignored by the painter and do not seem to have prevented purchase by eighteenth-century buyers. Some of the figures and many of the domestic pieces were of original design, and the latter sometimes took the form of overlapping leaves (Fig. 90), or embodied other vegetable forms.

A noticeably deep and strong blue was used, and this was overpainted occasionally with a thick white instead of the more usual gilding. Most pieces were left unmarked, but a small proportion bear two crossed 'L's' with three dots below in blue.

90. Sauceboat designed as a group of cabbage leaves with a twig handle. About 1755. 8½ inches long.

91. Tankard, painted in blue, with a Chinese figure holding a parasol. About 1755. 4 inches high.

92. Cup, painted in colours, with architecturally-improbable buildings of a kind often found on Longton Hall pieces. About 1755. 2½ inches high.

93. Pug-dog decorated under the glaze in blue and brown. About 1755. 3¾ inches high.

94. A girl dancing, her skirt painted in red stripes giving a vivid sense of movement. About 1755. 6¼ inches high.

95. Harlequin as a bagpiper. About 1755. 5¼ inches high.

96. A boy holding flowers and wearing a garland on his head, perhaps symbolising Summer. About 1755. 4¼ inches high.

97. Hercules and the Lion, the separate (but original) stand painted with a Chinese scene. About 1755. $7\frac{3}{4}$ inches high over-all.

LIVERPOOL

In 1756 one of the principal workmen at Worcester was engaged to start a factory at Liverpool, and it can come as no surprise to learn that there is a strong resemblance between many of the wares from both places; both used Cornish soapstone as an ingredient. The porcelain from this factory, and from others in the city, is not of notably high quality; much was painted in blue and some in other colours, but without any great distinction of design or execution.

A large proportion of the output was exported to America and the West Indies, and doubtless was turned out in quantity to sell cheaply. None of the Liverpool factories used marks, and only in recent years has research decided what was made there, but problems still remain unsolved.

Liverpool was known also for the decoration of both pottery and porcelain with printed patterns, and from about 1760 a flourishing business was done in performing this service for Wedgwood and other makers (Fig. 15).

98. Sauceboat with blue printed decoration, the handle ending in a snake's head. About 1770. $7\frac{1}{2}$ inches long.

99. Tall vase and cover with exotic birds painted in colours. About 1760. 15½ inches high. Such strange-looking birds were a popular subject with most factories. They were European versions of those on imported Oriental ware, which often had their origin in mythology rather than Nature.

100. Milk jug and a pair of
pickle-trays or sweetmeat
dishes decorated with
flowers in blue. About
1770. Jug, 4¾ inches high.

101. Teapot with moulded
and blue-painted
decoration. About 1770.
7 inches high.

LOWESTOFT

This East Anglian factory was opened in 1757, and it is said that one of the partners was smuggled into the Bow works so that he could learn their secrets. Certainly, the two wares bear a strong resemblance to one another; not only are they alike in the porcelain itself, but both favoured painting in blue.

The Lowestoft factory has acquired a greater fame than its productions merit from having had its name given to a type of Chinese eighteenth-century porcelain made for export to the West. The story of its alleged English origin was told in a book published a hundred years ago, and although soon discredited the name 'Lowestoft' continues often to be applied to this Oriental ware.

True English Lowestoft was confined principally to domestic pieces, and although a few figures were made they cannot be claimed to have much interest. A proportion of the output was painted with names or initials and dates, many referring to local persons, which gives it a wider appeal than would otherwise be the case (Figs 102 and 106).

102 and 103. Inkwell with a spray of flowers, painted in blue, and *below* the inscribed base. 2⅞ inches diameter.

104. Saucer with a dragon, painted in blue. About 1775. 5⅛ inches diameter.

105. Milk jug with an Oriental pattern painted in various colours. About 1775. 3 inches high.

106. Teapot painted in
colours and inscribed:
'Maria Hoyle NORWICH
1774'. 6½ inches high.

107. Cup and saucer
painted with flowers in
pink within a gilt border.
Part of a teaset made for
Robert Browne, one of the
partners in the factory, for
his wedding-day. About
1775. Saucer, 5 inches
diameter.

CAUGHLEY

Thomas Turner, who had been employed at Worcester, began to make porcelain at Caughley (pronounced 'Coffley'), near Broseley, Shropshire, in about 1772. Early wares are like those of Worcester, but if held to the light Caughley is yellow or brown in tone, in contrast to the green tone of Worcester. Much was decorated in blue, either by hand-painting or printing, and among popular designs used there was numbered the well-known 'Willow Pattern', supposed to have been engraved first by Turner's pupil, Thomas Minton. No figures were made.

Marks used were a capital 'C' (for Caughley), which is mistaken sometimes for the Worcester crescent, an 'S' (for Salopian or Shropshire), and SALOPIAN impressed.

108. Dish with a pierced border and twig handles, and with printed and painted patterns in blue. Marked with a capital 'C'. About 1785. 10¾ inches long.

109. Sauceboat with moulded and blue-painted decoration, marked with a capital 'S'. About 1780. 4 inches long.

110. Cream jug printed in blue with a Chinese pattern and marked with a capital 'S'. About 1785. 7 inches long.

PLYMOUTH AND BRISTOL

111. William Cookworthy, 1705–1780, painted by John Opie, R.A.

The researches of a Plymouth chemist, William Cookworthy (Fig. 111), resulted in the making of the only true hard-paste porcelain in England; made in the same manner as that imported from the Far East from a mixture of china-stone and china-clay. It needed a very high temperature for successful firing and this necessitated long experiment, but by 1768 a factory had been opened. This lasted only two years and in 1770 the enterprise was transferred to Bristol.

At Plymouth, the ware was often misshapen, stained from smoke in the kiln and flawed by cracks, but in spite of innumerable difficulties much of the output was excellent. A proportion was painted in blue, often blackish in tone, with Oriental scenes which were popular also on coloured pieces. Figures were made and some of the models were both original and attractive (Fig. 116).

After the move to Bristol, many pieces were based on French patterns and decoration was often fashionably showy with much gilding. Figures, tablewares of all kinds and large vases were produced. In 1781 the company was sold to a group of Staffordshire potters (Fig. 121), and the production of porcelain ceased in the West Country.

112. Sauceboat painted in colours, and marked in red with the sign for Tin. About 1770.
6¼ inches long.

The mark used at Plymouth was the alchemist's sign for Tin, like a figure 4 with a curled front $\mathbf{4}$
upright. It was also used for a time at Bristol, where they preferred later a cross in blue or gold or
a capital 'B'. As the sign for Tin was employed at both places it is often difficult to decide whether
a particular piece was made before or after the move. Much of the ware from both factories, as from
many others, was unmarked, but in the case of Plymouth and Bristol it can be recognised after a
little experience by its distinctive hard paste.

113. Cup and saucer painted in blue with an Oriental pattern, and marked in blue with the
sign for Tin. About 1770. Saucer, $6\frac{1}{4}$ inches diameter.

114. Teapot painted in colours and inscribed under the base: 'Mr. Wm. Cookworthy's Factory Plymouth 1770'. 5¼ inches high.

115. A mortar, painted in blue and marked with the sign for Tin. About 1770. 4 inches high.

116. Group of a boy with a dolphin on a base encrusted with sea-shells and coral. About 1770. 10 inches high.

117. Vase with moulded and painted decoration. About 1770. 12¼ inches high.

118. Figure of a milkmaid and a goat-herd. About 1775. $10\frac{1}{2}$ and 11 inches high.

119. Tureen and cover painted in colours. About 1775. 5¼ inches high.

120. Small bowl painted with an Oriental pattern in colours. About 1800. 4½ inches diameter.   121. Milk jug painted in colours. About 1800. 4 inches high. The men who purchased the Bristol factory closed it and made a quantity of simply-decorated wares from the same formula at the New Hall factory in Staffordshire. In due course they adopted a soft-paste porcelain from which the typical pieces shown above were made.

EARLY NINETEENTH CENTURY

One of the most beautiful porcelains ever made anywhere came from Wales between 1813 and 1822 at Nantgarw and Swansea. The material was white and translucent, and much of it was sold undecorated to be painted in London in the most delicate manner (Figs 122 and 123).

The Derby and Worcester factories made wares of high quality in the fashionable Classical style (Figs 124 to 127), and the Coalport factory, which absorbed those of Caughley and Nantgarw, made well-finished pieces for a large public (Fig. 126). At the Rockingham works, at Swinton in Yorkshire, and in Staffordshire, were factories that catered for those who liked realistic miniature models of dogs (Fig. 131) and homes (Fig. 132); the latter ranging from turreted castles to rose-festooned cottages in which perfume-pastilles might be burned. At Rockingham were made also numerous dessert-services and vases decorated profusely in the taste of the time.

Josiah Spode and his sons had a flourishing factory in Staffordshire where high quality wares were made (Fig. 129), and after being bought by a partner, William Taylor Copeland, in 1833, continues to manufacture to-day under the latter name. Worcester and Mintons (Fig. 130), the latter founded at the very end of the eighteenth century, are also still in production.

122. Swansea spill-vase decorated in gold and dark brown, marked under the base with the name of a firm of dealers PELLATT & GREEN LONDON in red. About 1815. 5¼ inches high.

123. Plate painted with roses, decorated with gilding and bearing the impressed mark NANTGARW C W (the latter for China Works). About 1815. 9¼ inches diameter.

124. Worcester beaker painted in colours within blue and gold borders, and marked with an incised capital 'B' for Flight and Barr. About 1805. 4 inches high.

125. Derby plate with a group of birds painted in colour within a gilt border, marked with crossed batons, dots and a crown in red. About 1810. 8¾ inches diameter.

126. Two-handled mug, or loving-cup, with painted views of Oxford and heavily gilded. Under the base are the names of the views: 'Oxford from the Meadows' and 'Oxford from Iffley'. Probably Coalport, about 1830. 10½ inches long.

127. Worcester cup, cover and stand with feathers painted in colours on a salmon-pink and gilt ground. Probably Chamberlain's factory, about 1810. Stand, $5\frac{5}{8}$ inches diameter.

128. Worcester cup and saucer, each in the shape of a tulip and the former with a gilded butterfly handle. Impressed mark FBB, for Flight, Barr and Barr. About 1820. Saucer, $4\frac{1}{4}$ inches diameter.

129. Spode vase with painted flowers in colours on a dark blue and gold ground. Marked in red SPODE 1166; the latter is the number of the pattern. About 1820. 4¾ inches high. 130. Mintons vase painted in colours with purple-striped double anemones, marked with double 'L' above 'M' in blue. About 1815. 4¾ inches high.

131. Rockingham poodle on a royal-blue cushion. About 1825. 4¾ inches long. 132. Pastille-burner in the form of a cottage. Probably Staffordshire, about 1830. 3¼ inches high.